MW01251635

The Fifth Ace

by

Iris Banister, M.S., ED.

GTNN Press • Rochester • New York

First printing, January 1995
GARVEY-TUBMAN-NANNY-NZINGA Press
GTNN Press
Rochester, New York 14611
(716) 464-0694

Library of Congress Catalog Card Number: 95-81655
ISBN: 0-9640639-7-2

TABLE OF CONTENTS

ACKNOWLEDGEMENTS

I would like to take this opportunity to publicly thank the many students who participated in the data gathering process for this book.

Special thanks to the host of teachers, parents and school administrators of the Rochester, Albany, Detroit and Brooklyn School Districts for their support and encouragement to put this data and ideas into writing. It is my hope that this book has captured the essence of your intentions that caused you to insist that I write it, NOW!

Thomas, Tommy, Simeon and Ethan, my wonderful and generous family...thank you for being who you are. Thanks for the lack of complaint about less than delicious, full meals, missed events, late laundry, few sleep-overs, and quick reads of your homework. You were and remain precious.

Thanks to my friend and colleague, Paul Brainwien, who took the challenge to illustrate the cover of this book. It is great and clearly delivers the message, The Fifth Ace!

Finally, thanks to all the educators and laymen for the wealth of invaluable feedback. Your constructive criticism and stick-to-it attitude was the inspiration that motivated me to complete this work.

Dedication

To Professor Harold Munson, who said, "Go home and write"; and I did.
Thanks!

INTRODUCTION

INTRODUCTION

Consider it safe to say that the majority of students (regardless of age or grade) come to school with a preconceived idea as to how and what it will be. These ideas are based on both fiction and nonfiction. Some ideas are a collage of bits and pieces of stories that they have overheard or been told directly at home, by friends, and neighbors. Some of the ideas are the fruits of an active imagination. No matter what the source of the ideas, they represent the reality of the student.

It must be noted that the imagery surrounding school has changed drastically since the late 1970's. Most urban children prior to the late 1970's imagined school to be a wonderland where a wonderful thing called learning happened to them. School was thought to be a place filled with fun and excitement; a place where students were treated with kindness and where everybody was glad that they were there. There was this person who ruled the wonderland who was fashioned in their minds as a "fairy Godmother", and in some rare cases a "fairy Godfather". This person was called "teacher." The teacher was the one who assured that all went well with the girls and boys. The teacher was in charge of making sure that each girl and boy got that thing called education. They thought that they went into wonderland not knowing very much and came out knowing how to read, write, and do numbers.

For a host of reasons (social, political, and economical, which will not be discussed here) the image of school as a wonderland among urban pre-schoolers changed. The image of school changed to being thought of as a vast wilderness froth with danger, and with a landlord who is cruel and very uncaring. Some see school as a prison where students are forced to go daily. The prison has a Warden (principal) and a hierarchical guard system. Teachers are the lowest level of this prison guard system; therefore they are the most unsatisfied. They are thus seen as the most cruel members in the system. The image of school as a prison, armed camp, wilderness, and other such descriptions are so pervasive that urban children getting ready to attend school for the first time are filled with fear and apprehension. The old joy and excitement have given way to these images; thus school is not a positively anticipated event for these children. The wonderful thing called learning that the boys and girls feel has very little value when their very lives may be in danger. Children turned their attention from learning to survival. So begins the preparation of getting mentally ready to go to school (and to go back to school) which causes great nervousness and fear in students.

Many urban children feel that they must come to school prepared to defend themselves from teachers and other unknown predators that may be disguised as well-meaning people. This preparation is just so that they can survive the school experience. Some students are conscious of their preparation; thus they come to school with their guards up and are ready to react in the blink of an eye. The choice of the reaction(s) in the survival modality is the reflection of the child's urban experiences. These reactions or tactics range from the silent staring method, cursing, smart retorts, and the ultimate physical attack (fighting). In the cases when a tactic is needed, the student is the sole judge as to which one is appropriate for the given situation. Other students are totally not conscious of their preparation for school. These students are usually shocked themselves when they react in the tactics of the urban survival modality. These students are either repulsed by their behavior and seek out other means of reacting or feel an exhilaration of power and control. This feeling of empowerment often causes them to continue in the survival modality.

In a class of twenty-eight to thirty-three students, there are some who have the wonderland view (these students usually are those who have met with school success academically and/or come from homes that truly have sent the message that education is good and is a means of securing a prosperous future). There will be students in that class who have the prison view of school. In the minds of these students there is an automatic: "Them", (school staff, especially teachers) and "Me", system that is activated by school attendance. There will also be students who see school as a wilderness. The wilderness view suggests a survival of the fittest, or an

"I'd better get you before you get me" mind set. In this same class there will be students who don't neatly fit into either of these points of view. These students are neither fish nor fowl, they come to school not committed to any particular view of school that can be considered a set of tactics. These students are not totally immune to the influence of others and usually develop their own school coping mechanism. This mechanism does not necessarily ingratiate them with some of their peers or their teacher(s). These students are usually sure of the need for personal survival in school. This type of student is also susceptible to embracing either of the behavior modalities present in the class.

Neither of these methods employed by students when reacting to school circumstances are within themselves necessarily negative. How teachers and schools pre-plan and react to the behaviors exhibited by students is the determining factor of success for students and teachers (schools). Pre-knowledge of the very existence of these various views held by urban students of school maximizes the ability of school communities and more especially teachers, to provide proper learning opportunities for students. What is not known has far more of a potential for negative consequences than having the advantage of at least being aware. "KNOWING is a giant step toward educating." To reap the full benefit of this book, keep that thought upper most in your mind.

The major purposes of this publication are: the opening of the urban school doors to those seeking insight into the motivating factors relative to the actions and reactions of students; as well as to offer some simple techniques to educators in an effort to assist them in the task of educating their students. It must be understood by the reader that there is no definite set of explanations for the motives of urban children. There are recurring actions and reactions by students with consistent rationales gleaned from students that have allowed for the development of reasonable hypotheses. Some hypotheses have been tested (over a 20 year span of time), and those results are presented in this book as discussions and recommendations. Collegial advice might be a better description of the intended purpose of the recommendations.

The title "The Fifth Ace", is somewhat of an inside joke that has been acted out over twenty-five years of working as a professional educator in urban schools. The punch line is being in a situation (in school with students) where you know that you have played every card in your deck of "Things To Do When..." and wishing that you had just one more ace (one more effective technique) to play. Inevitably, if you think long and hard enough, you will be surprised to find up your sleeve, behind your back, somewhere, that fifth ace. There is always one more way to reach your students. After the official four aces are played, there is always the "Fifth Ace."

A group of teachers were in the faculty room sharing some of their greatest feats of the day. There were stories about all kinds of humorous and serious situations. One teacher told about the student who refused to do work in class. To that student's amazement the teacher called the parent during the class. Well, after a few words from Mom on the phone, the student found that the classwork was exactly what he wanted to do. One story told by a teacher was about a student complaining about having to do homework. The teacher laughed almost uncontrollably, but managed to give us the punch line. The teacher assigned the student after school detention. Since the work was going to be done after school, it was no longer homework, but could now be considered post-school work. The student had to concede that the teacher had out-smarted him. The faculty room rocked with howls of laughter and an assortment of light-hearted comments. One teacher speaking in a very somber voice, informed the room that the students had clearly let him know that he had played all of his four aces (used all of his techniques). He went on to say how they had caught him at a loss for words and actions. There before his class, faced with the possibility of total exposure, naked before his students, his mind empty of "all things to do next," the teacher fell silent. Immediately teachers started to inquire as to what he had done to at least save face.

Then, for the first time I heard those most valuable words that led to the title of this book. The teacher said, "Little did they know, I had not played with a regulation deck. So I pulled out my Fifth Ace, and "WHAM!!", I won! I won the game. I got the last and final play. I was down, but not out! When I win this game, my students win because I am playing for them." The faculty room was filled with a pregnant silence. The bell rang for class, and everybody went their way just pondering that thought.

I hope that this book will give you some Fifth Ace techniques, or at least stir your creative juices to develop your own.

Chapter I

The Ceremonial Dance

THE CEREMONIAL DANCE

Experience has proven to educators that schools are nothing more than a microcosm of the real world. That real world is an amalgam of views of all those who comprise the school community. Therefore, schools cannot, should not, pretend that the real life issues faced by students are not a part of their school life. The whole child comes to school. Parts of that wholeness are all of the experiences (good and bad, negative and positive) that the child has had to the point in time when he/she walks into the school. To ignore or not validate these experiences or to treat them in ways that would suggest that they are less than real is like saying to the child that certain aspects of her/his existence (or maybe his/her whole life) has no value. The resulting message to the student is that he/she is not accepted or acceptable to the teacher (school). Not to legitimize or affirm the experiences that students divulge to the teacher (school) either directly or indirectly, is in fact to negate the relevance of the child as a complete wholesome individual. The most common reaction of urban children is to find some reason as to why the teacher (school) is less than accepted or acceptable to them. They have a whole arsenal of reasons at their ready disposal and will use them automatically. Many students already believe that teachers (school) feel and think of them as not quite right (inadequate).

One goal, then, of the urban school community (every adult who represents the school: administration, bus drivers, cafeteria staff, custodians, security staff, etc.) and every teacher in the school, should be to bring the feeling of total acceptance/acceptability to every student as a part of the normal school experience. Normal is emphasized because urban children are accustomed to programs that are designed to HELP them fit into some system or the other. Schools should make every effort not to be viewed by students as are these programs.

It has been said that urban children of school age live in two worlds. They live in these two worlds not by choice but rather by happenstance. Students look for, but rarely speak about, the need to merge these two worlds into one existence; a single existence where they are welcome because they belong. Schools in urban centers must make every effort to provide students the support necessary to merge their "out-of-school self" and their "in-school self." The merger sought is the one "self" that brings the child a sense of personal integration.

Too often urban students at every grade level say that they feel the need to become someone other than their "home self" just to become a part of the school culture. In the earlier grades more often than not, the "school self" takes on those attributes that students believe are acceptable to teachers. This "school self" is supposed to afford the child ready acceptance, being interpreted by the child as success in school. The "school self" will learn to read, behave properly, and be well liked by all. The "school self" must be careful not to reflect any quality from the "out-of-school self" because it is sure to cause conflict for the "in-school self." Consequently, these little urban elementary children are making a conscious effort to rid themselves of any "out-of-school self" actions (which they consider negative) and at the same time are trying to define and exhibit a "school self" that will assure them a place of acceptance and success given by the teacher. Students believe that acceptance from the teacher is the ultimate prize which will secure success for them. A simple smile, a little word of encouragement, a brush of the hair, or a light pat on the back serve as indicators to students that the "school self" is working.

It is unfortunate that these children so believe in the need to have a "school self" that they will make up stories about the "out-of-school self". The intent is to make it appear that the "real self" is the one who comes to school. These stories sometimes cause children to not want parents, family members, or anyone familiar to come to school. They fear that the "school self" will be discovered by someone who knows the "real self" (the out-of-school self"). In the minds of these little children, school visits by family members or home visits by teachers represent a natural collision between their two worlds. In some cases, the students fall on the mercy of the teacher to ignore the discrepancy between what they had tried to portray by the "school self" and the "out-of-school self." In other cases, the child may feel a sense of exposure and decide to assassinate the "school self" by letting the "out-of-school self" (the "real self") come to school in place of the "school self." In these instances it may seem to the teacher that the child is as different as night and day. The "new" child is usually rebellious, rude, uncooperative, and shows overt disdain for school. Some children react to this perceived exposure by becoming withdrawn, silent, sullen, and even introverted. The child believes that "the school self" has failed, and that he/she is no longer accepted/acceptable to the teacher. The teacher probably shows no signs of change toward the child. It does not matter to the child because his/her reality built on experience tells him/her that exposure means rejection. Rare is the child who is not affected by the teacher discovering the other world where the "out-of-school self" lives.

Another disaster waiting to happen in regard to the two worlds of "self" within urban children is the possibility of failure. If the idea of adopting a "school self" is to garner acceptance from the teacher which is manifested through school success, then what happens to the children who are not academically successful? The reactions of these children are in many cases the same as those associated with the exposure of the "out-of-school self", but the motivation this time is betrayal. Students believe that the teacher did not live up to her/his part of the bargain. The two prevalent reactions are: the teacher as a betrayer; the student thinks, "I hate you (teacher) because you hate me." The second reaction is the "I knew it all the time" or the "I knew it was going to happen"; - fulfillment of prophecy. At this point, the idea of the teacher being a racist is more than likely going to surface (this is not based on race; it does not matter if you are white, black or a member of any other ethnic or cultural group). If not racist then perhaps the explanation will be because the teacher is sexist. You don't like boys (girls), or you like boys (girls) better than girls (boys). (The sex of the teacher does not matter). It is important to note that whichever explanation the student chooses to explain failure, it will usually be embraced by parents (guardians) as having some validity. There are instances where parents not only find validity in the explanation of their children for failing or being in trouble, but readily accept it as total truth (based on their own notions about schools and teachers). Failure in school takes away the hope and pride with which children came to school and parents (guardians) sent them to school. These positive emotions are replaced with frustration and fear by both the child and the parent. They usually direct those negative emotions at the teacher. The belief is that surely there must be something that the teacher can do to make things better for the child; or something that the teacher should have done; or maybe it is something that the teacher did not do that resulted in student failure! These are the constant refrains of parents and other interested parties. These conclusions are considered to be reasonable by other parents who are in similar situations or those who simply empathize with these parents. The bottom line is that students and parents believe that teachers deserve the blame for student failure. They also believe that teachers deserve the major part of the compliments for student success. If students are successful (as defined by parents) then the teacher is described as a good teacher who cares about the students. If the students fail, the teacher is said to be a poor (bad) teacher who doesn't care about the students, and is only there for the money, the paycheck.

Until about the fifth grade, most students will continue trying to construct and reconstruct a "school self." The motivation, according to students surveyed, is the effort to become acceptable to the teacher which will insure school success. Even in the face of continued failure, some of the students report that they continue to try a new construct or a new approach to the "school self." It is simply because they like school and believe that they can find that perfect "school self." Fifth graders usually make a conscious decision to drop this "school self" and abandon all attempts at trying to construct a "new self." They come to the conclusion that it is not worth the pain and constant rejection they feel as a part of the school experience. They decide to just be "real" and declare that, "I am what I am, like it or not. Take a good look; this is me." Children who are meeting with success in school tend to continue in the "school self" modality, providing their sense of acceptance by the school is of high value to them. The decision to show the "real self" is many times caused by peer pressure. The old "you are trying to be white" accusation from peers has been responsible for many students giving up the struggle for a "school self" or causing students to stop trying for success in school. The "You ain't down with the crew" comment has taken its number of students out of the struggle for a "school self" or away from school success. The more important the opinions of peers, the more likely it is that students will yield. Common also among urban fifth graders is the belief that they have arrived at the size and age when they must be responsible for their personal survival. Students are convinced in their minds that in order to survive in school and out of school they had better be more reflective of those who dominate both communities. Teachers and the acceptance that they represent are no longer of major importance. Teachers are not an intricate part of the equation in making the decision to stop the struggle for a "school self." Students feel that when they were younger they were more dependent on the teacher; therefore, he/she played a big part in their decision making (teachers are not asked to give an opinion, the students assume what teachers want from them based on their experiences both in school and out of school), but now that the student is older and more independent, he/she makes the decision alone.

In most cases these urban fifth graders rarely seek the advice of parents as to whether they should stop the struggle for a "school self." Parents have reported that they were not only unaware of a change in a "self," but were not aware that their children had even been in such a struggle. Students at this age start to exercise more independence in regard to school. At the same time, vast numbers of parents tend to remove themselves from a great deal of regular involvement in school. In the face of less parent involvement and more independence, the student is fairly free to explore a multiplicity of different "selves" to live out in school.

The current trend among urban students (more especially fifth grade and higher) is for them to establish an out of school "public self" which becomes the reputation for which they are known no matter what the place or circumstances. The school now is just another stage on which that reputation can be played and enhanced. These reputations can be anything from some movie idol to a super star jock, or street smart/wise guy, or a "gangsta rappa," or a deep, profound revolutionary, or a nerd, or a weird outsider, and on, and on, and on. The limitations of developing a reputation are only governed by the minds of the children who are the designers. This process of selecting and developing a reputation is equally true for boys and girls.

Reputations sometimes are given to students because of something that they have done or said which was significant enough for it to stick. Sometimes the reputation is a nickname that the student was given affectionately by a family member that takes on new meaning when used on the street and in school. It is not to be readily assumed that a reputation is indicative of a negative or problem child. Some of the reputations are innocent and carry no particular threat, while other reputations are intended as a warning. Urban students, unlike other students, perhaps, realize that a respected reputation can serve as a suit of armor, or at best help move them towards more acceptance among their peers. If the reputation is innocuous, there is little or no need for concern for the school community. Usually there are large numbers of students with reputations. Those who want reputations in urban schools at any cost do pose a need for concern for the school. Some of these reputations have been and can be earned through acts of violence, mean-spirited verbal attacks, and other negative antisocial behaviors. For most students who desire to keep these gained reputations, it often means a continuation of whatever it took to get the reputation in the first place. These types of reputations do in varying degrees impact the school community (especially the classroom) in negative ways.

RECOMMENDATIONS

- Knowing is your most valuable commodity. In the first few days of school, devise a method that will help you gain as much knowledge about each of your students as possible (i.e., a survey, group activities, questionnaires, Tell Me games, etc.)

- Urban children react particularly well to adults who not only ask them questions about themselves, but who are also willing to share personal information with them about the adult. Without being too personal, share information about yourself that tells them more about who you "really" are beyond being the teacher. This will help dismiss the idea of you being a perfect person or in some way unreal (the belief of teachers being non-people allows students to treat them in ways that they would not treat someone they considered to be a real, live person, not too unlike themselves).

- Types of information that you might want to share may include, but not be limited to:
  - * Your nickname (reputation)
  - * Where you are from (be sure to include what brought you to this place)

* Describe yourself as a student (grammar school - college)
* Your family structure (marital status, children, pets, etc.)
* How and why you became a teacher - why this school
* Some of your personal goals
* Your rebellious days (be careful, tell it in a therapeutic manner that will show the possibility for positive change).

- As you question and share with your students, be sure to allow yourself to be open to their questions. Exercise wisdom; every question posed does not necessarily have to be answered. However, every question asked should be addressed. These activities will help you send the unspoken message to your students that you care and are concerned about each of them as a whole person - all "selves" included. It is not that they care that you know, but that they know that you care.

- Parents are your best allies. Get to them as soon as possible. Even before school starts, take the opportunity to call them. Be brave enough to ask them for the opportunity to meet them either at their homes, in the school, or even in a neutral place. Parents often report of never hearing from the teacher personally until there is trouble with their children. Don't let that be said about you. Be pro-active. Make the first positive steps toward forging a partnership. It will serve you well to do so.

- In the first few days of school you want to make sure your students know that you are all beginning this adventure toward knowledge at the same point. That point is at ***together*** (in this class we are starting together). Help them to believe that your job is to make sure that at the end of the school year each of them knows more in all areas of study than they did at the beginning. Challenge them; tell them that if they will cooperate with you and their fellow classmates, like the Staple Singers or Greyhound Bus declare, "You'll get them there!"

- Be sure to give your students a rendition of, "there will perhaps be setbacks and disappointments along the way - but we'll go through them together!!!" This goes a long way in setting the stage for trust. Be certain that you really mean it because they will bring it back to your remembrance from time to time.

- The higher the grade level of your students the more important it is to have the "I used to be" and the "I used to think" conversation with your class and at times with individual students (trust yourself, you'll know the right time and the right students). You will use these conversations when you have noted a marked change (negative or positive) in your class or individual students. This is your reality check to learn where your students' minds are as well as a reality check to help them know that you are on top of things - all of the time (A Fifth Ace).

The Ceremonial Dance is one of the most valuable acts you'll perform because it is that smooth, deliberate means that will help you to know your students and in turn help them get to know you. The dance usually lasts in the formal stage, for two to five days at the very start (first day) of the school year. Timing is crucial as with any dance done with partners. The informal aspect of the dance actually continues throughout the whole school year. The value of this ceremonial dance should not be underestimated.

Of course, you will have limited time during the first few days of school due to all of the clerical and bookkeeping chores that you must get done to make sure that your teaching gets off to a professional start. I would suggest to you that the long term value of the ceremonial dance (sharing and exchanging knowing one another - student and teacher) will be pivotal to every success you make with your students.

Urban students have come to expect the unexcited, book-oriented, cold opening of school; no ceremonial dance. This is your opportunity to pleasantly surprise your students, and reap future benefits for yourself. So here is your invitation. Dance that dance and keep on dancing!

Chapter II

The Push and Pull

THE PUSH AND PULL

It is a fact that a large number of urban school children come from homes that are headed by a single parent (usually the mother) and on the average have at least two to three children. Older children or the oldest child play roles in the family that are usually reserved for adults. Many of the boys are referred to as "the man of the house" regardless of their age. Girls are the recipients of titles such as "little mama", "my little lady", and "woman-girl". Comments like, "He is more man as a boy than his daddy is right now," or "This little girl thinks that she's the mother around here," are often used to describe these children. Such remarks are interpreted by these youngsters to mean that they are more than just children and have special rights to act and respond in adult-like ways. These children often find themselves in charge of other siblings and household responsibilities (i.e., cooking, cleaning, securing the house at night, television selection for all viewers, etc.). There are probably instances when they are in absolute control for short periods of time when the responsible adult is away. There may even be times when they find themselves in complete charge for long, extended periods. In either case, they may be unaware as to the whereabouts of the person who is normally responsible for the care of the dwelling (Note: These situations are not restricted to urban areas).

This kind of awesome responsibility placed on young children (school age) is not an uncommon set of events. It is a scene that is played out over and over again in urban areas. The scourge of drugs, poor economic status, the changing values of society, and the breakdown of the family bear blame for the negative situations faced by many urban households. Single parents are forced to enter the job market and (or) onto welfare rolls. Welfare in a large majority of instances is inadequate, creating a need to augment the family's income by working. Children find themselves having to sacrifice their childhood. They must accept roles of greater responsibility than their suburban counterparts.

Schools are directly affected by this type of home situation in that children who are semi-heads of households or who almost totally bear the responsibility for themselves, come to school not seeing themselves as children. They see themselves, in a real sense as more than children, but less than adults. They have acted in adult roles long enough to feel that they have earned the right to not be treated as mere children.

Now think for a moment. If these children come to school thinking of themselves as almost equal to adults or even as adult-like in experience, then it is logical to believe that they are not going to tolerate being treated the way that schools (teachers) normally treat children. This is not meant to necessarily be an indictment of the treatment that students receive in urban schools (that is a topic for another book).

These children have every right to expect to be treated differently; after all, they have been for the better part of their lives (some longer than others) the persons in charge, acting out adult roles. To solidify their perceived notions of adulthood status, they are often told by parents and significant others that they are very mature, act older than their age would presume, and that they are smart and act just like they are grown. They are told that they do not have to take anything off of anybody because they can handle themselves.

That advice even extends to the school. They are told "if the teacher or anybody else treats you mean, in a rude fashion, or harshly, you don't have to take it. Stand up for yourself, you are a person, too" (not just these children are given this type of advice, but other children tend to act it out differently in school. They act out this advice in ways more like you would expect children to behave).

Behavior management for the teacher when dealing with these "more than children" students has the potential to become a battle of wills better known as the PUSH AND PULL. The more the teacher tries to push the child (no matter how gently) towards childlike behavior, the more the child will pull the attention of the class and the teacher way from academics, thus giving him/her control. The teacher fully understands that he/she is responsible for the whole class and ultimately must determine the "what," "when" and "how" for the class. The "more than a child" student does not understand that when in school he/she is expected to yield the adult-like status to the actual adult, the teacher. Thus, the opportunity for conflict presents itself when the student feel that his/her "rights" are being pulled away. The action of the student is to assert (push) himself/herself and demand equality. It is incumbent upon the teacher to identify the Push and Pull process and diminish it as much as possible. The wise teacher must have personal issues around control and the role of a child resolved before tackling this type of student. The teacher must be able to support the needs of this child and at the same time help the child to find acceptance.

It is very important for the teacher to know his/her leadership style. Teaching is usually done through one's style of leadership. Let's explore this point for a moment. A teacher with an autocratic leadership style may see children as mostly empty vessels, inexperienced, and in awe of adults, ready to accept them as the total and final authority. The laissez-faire type teacher may see children as little people, free moral agents who should be viewed by adults as raw potential. This potential must be allowed to develop into fully franchised people (adults) through gentle prodding and guidance. The democratic style teacher may see children as joint architects in their growth and development with the adult as the model and an assistant.

Each of these leadership styles has merit and can be appropriate in the classroom. There is no right or wrong style of leadership for one to be a good teacher. The key is not the style of leadership, but rather that the teacher is wise enough to let whatever his/her style is become an asset. Through the leadership style of the teacher, the child must be made to feel empowered, nurtured, and accepted. No one style of leadership works better with this particular child ("more than a child" student) than with any other type of child. Each style, when used in a child-centered approach, can be effective. For example:

- The autocratic teacher and this type of student may be in continual conflict.

- The laissez-faire teacher may send the message that the student is stronger than he/she which causes the student to take liberties beyond the purview of a student.

- The democratic teacher may lead the student to believe that they are equals. When the teacher really wants to be in charge, the student will not relent and may become resentful towards the teacher.

On the other hand, each of the leadership styles may be of great effect when faced with this type of student. Consider these examples:

- The autocratic teacher may help these students to see a new way to behave that is more child-like which highlights the rewards of childhood. This may relieve the child from the burden of acting like an adult and lead to the enjoyment of just being a "kid." Or perhaps the autocratic teacher will assist the student in exhibiting those adult-like qualities in the way he/she approaches assignments and manages time.

- The laissez-faire teacher may provide enough time for the student to recognize a need for adult support in setting limits which causes the child to see the difference between mature adults and children who have assumed adult roles. As a result of the laissez-faire style, the child may reach out to the teacher for security which helps him/her grasp the child within.

- Perhaps the democratic teacher who allows the student to work closely as a partner may show skills and knowledge beyond that of the student, moving the student to realize that he/she does not have all that is needed to truly be an adult. That reality frees the child to act in ways that are more like a child.

I'm sure as a teacher (or one who works with urban youth) reading this, that a number of different techniques have come to your mind and already you are working with this child in your spirit.

What is vital to remember is that it is not your style of leadership, but rather that you are an effective leader (teacher) for all of your students. What is your intent in dealing with difficult or differently oriented children is the question to pose to yourself. Do you desire to educate or dominate? If dominate is your answer, get ready to PUSH AND PULL. If your intent is to educate, you can put yourself in the position to touch students in such a way that they will permit you to teach them. Teaching is by permission, and learning is by will.

RECOMMENDATIONS

- In your "Getting To Know You" methodology (Chapter 1), be sure to ask questions or provide opportunity for students to share a bit of their family history (frame it in such a way that it includes family structure). Knowing is half the battle!

- Be comfortable with your teaching style. Don't try to change your style to accommodate your "more than children" students. Know that you must use your style in such a way that you will present yourself as a friend, rather than a foe or competitor.

- You must make every effort to be clear (very clear) with your students about the way you see your role as the teacher and their role as students. The "more than children" will usually surface at this juncture. They will usually give you indicators as to whether they agree with your description of each role. Be alert to body language, facial expressions, and barely audible comments that usually generate laughter from the other students.

- To be successful with this type of student (most students) don't judge or evaluate negatively the information that these students share with you about their home life. If you choose to give assistance through proper channels or seek help for the student and the family, be certain that the student first agrees to your help and then quickly make contact with the home to get agreement or further input. (Note: For those things that you are required by law to report to the proper authorities, do so without hesitation. If you are unsure, check with an authority in the school. Someone will know or will be able to help you find someone who knows the correct procedure). Make sure you explain your lawful duty to the student and the parent. Remember, you must do what is required.

- Fortify yourself because it may be difficult for you, but don't remind these students ("more than children") that they are children and not adults. Believe me, you are usually touching a sensitive, private area (they usually harbor some resentment for having been put in this adult role, and they have probably been told numerous times that they are not adults). They do not need to hear this from you who is supposed to be the empathetic other. You do not need to bring this kind of grief to yourself or risk polarizing the student(s).

- When you hear or see the manifestation of this "adult-like self" in your students, think of the most advantageous and empowering method (for your students and yourself) to address it. In most cases nothing said by the teacher may be the best way, but not always.

- Try to put yourself in the mental mind of this type of student (they usually represent a significant percentage of your students - elementary and secondary) before a confrontation. Keep them in mind as you plan your lessons and classroom activities.

- There is always value in making contact with the home before or to avoid the battle of the wills confrontation, PUSH AND PULL. There are usually answers or at least insights that you can get from a mere phone call to the home, or a visit for a friendly chit-chat (visits can take place at the home, places in the community, or by an invitation to the school). Like ET....phone home!

Chapter III

Eye To Eye

EYE TO EYE

Once a great opera singer was asked by a reporter how she avoided the various expressions on the faces of those in the audience. The opera singer answered that she located a spot just above the heads of the audience and always looked at that spot. A young teacher, having read this news article and a bit uncertain as to where she should look to avoid all the eyes of her fourth grade class, decided to take that advice. She got to school early that morning and located the spot in the room that she would look at to avoid having to turn her head like a security camera in a store while standing before the class. After about ten minutes of glancing at that spot, the young teacher realized that all of her fourth graders were now staring in the direction of the same spot. Finally, one brave student commented, "I know it seems that time will never pass, but it does, or Miss, is it that we are really that ugly?" All of the other students quickly agreed and let out a nervous laugh. Puzzled, it took the teacher a few minutes to realize that her focal point was on the same wall and at about the same level as the clock. Lesson: it's better to look like a roving security camera trying to look at each student than to have students believe that they are so ugly that you are waiting for that magic moment when you can flee from them.

Eye contact, body language and voice quality can make or break an urban educator. Yes, it does make a difference to your urban students how you look at them, move around and toward them, as well as the pitch, tone and volume of your voice. Most often, it is not what you say necessarily, but how you say it. I've witnessed teachers who have made very innocent and actually complimentary statements to students that were received with anger and resentment. When talking with the students to determine the source of their anger, it is usually that he/she (teacher) said this, this, and this. When you say to the children what's wrong with that, more chances than not they say in response, "...it is not just what he/she said, but how it was said." Something as simple as "did you hear what I said?" can cause some students to react in an aggressive and negative way or in a positive and constructive way, based on your voice. Not what you say, but how you say it, is the concept to remember.

The same holds true for body language. Urban students are taught almost as a sixth sense to read what someone is saying with the body as well as with the mouth. Body language plays a major role in the day-to-day life of urban children (especially African-American and Latino). To stand on any street corner in an urban neighborhood is to easily see the silent and continual conversations or messages sent without the use of verbal communication. It is clear who is in favor with whom, play time, pending danger, and a host of other situations can be identified. This same interpretation of body language (how one moves the body per the situation) is used when defining what the teacher "really" means or "actually" feels about an issue, a person or a situation. So strong is the student's reliance on body language that acceptance or rejection of the teacher can be based on it. "I don't like him/her." "Why?" "Look at how he/she acts, they ain't about nothing! I can tell that!" Conversations like that are classic examples of this point. An old common African-American saying which is appropriate here is "Your body is talking for you, so don't bother to open your mouth."

Eye contact is again a means by which urban students establish relationships or reject them. By merely the motion and set of the eyes, these young people determine the worth of giving respect, to challenge or not, to take seriously or not, and assign friendship or foe status. Failure to look at students directly in the eye can send a message that you are afraid of them, don't like them, or that you think they are inferior. A side view can be thought to be flirtatious, or say that you are untrustworthy, or that you are rolling your eyes at them which is a 'no no.' Rolling eyes is considered a challenge and a form of disrespect.

A discussion of eye contact, body language, and voice is not complete without a brief discussion about racism. This discussion is for Black, White, Latino, in fact any teacher who plans to teach in an urban school. Racism, perceived or real, is a factor in the lives of most urban children. Many of them have already, whether real or imagined, feel or felt that they have been or are the victims of racism. It is a common thought in inner city urban communities that schools are breeding grounds for racism. Many families, when believing that they can speak honestly, will admit to this belief and are able to share situations where it was indeed the case that they were the victims of racism.

A great number of urban students (especially beyond the fifth grade and often earlier) are certain in their ability to discover and clearly identify a racist by the way a person does or does not look at them, the way one walks or uses the hands and body, and finally by the very tone of the voice. We can look for scientific or even logical evidence to try and prove that urban children don't have that ability, but it would be to little or no avail. For this "knowing" has been passed through generations. It is a part of the survival skills taught either consciously or without deliberate conscious effort. Some argue that the very nature of the society that urban children grow up in teaches this skill. We will not take issue or position on that matter here, but we will as a matter of course, accept that these students believe that they have that ability. What this says to the teacher is important to this discussion. To this we say, know thyself and to thine own self be true. It is of great value for teachers to really know, (not think you know) what their true feelings are about race and culture, or if their stance will support them teaching in an urban school. Once they really know, they must determine if there is a need for further education or experiences to change their philosophical stance about race and culture. This might be the point when teachers realize that their stance prohibits them from teaching in an urban school. That is fine, just leave, nothing lost.

Remember this...if you let the fear of being labeled a racist define you, it will certainly defeat you.

RECOMMENDATIONS

- In your "Reality Check" methods (Chapter 1) take a gamble and broach the topic of racism, racist, and prejudice.

- Observe your students (regardless of grade) to try and determine their general concept of acceptable eye contact, body language, and voice level. It's worth the effort. It will probably be fun, and you might learn something new.

- Racism or the accusation of it hurts everybody. While you don't have to sleep or breathe it, you should at least be open and sensitive to the views and opinions of your students and their experiences. Be careful not to dismiss or ignore their realities (perceived or real).

- Grow a feeling of equality and belonging for all of your students as a part of the structure and physical layout of your room, your curriculum, and your interactions.

- Teaching is an art as well as a skill. Do not let yourself get so relaxed that you forget to practice both. You should always be aware of you. Your eyes, your total body and your voice are an intricate part of your craft.

- Remember...if you look for logic along racism's twisting, dimly lit passageways, you'll make yourself crazy. Racism just is, but it takes people to make it continue to be! Work at being the consummate professional.

- Your eyes, body and voice can secure your authority and prove your caring. Use them effectively to your advantage and that of your students.

Chapter IV

A $1,000,000 Smile

A $1,000,000 SMILE

It was a hard decision, but he had made up his mind. He was going to get that skin-tight fade haircut. His heart raced with every clip of the scissors. Beads of sweat formed on his forehead. It was very difficult parting with all that hair, but after all, his eighth graders had told him that it was time for him to get out of that time warp and come into the 21st century. Day after day of that same kind of conversation, the hinting, and the students almost pleading for him to do it, he thought he would surprise them Monday morning. It took some getting used to, but after seeing himself in the mirror about a million times, he concluded that the kids were right. "I've come out of the past, and I look good," he told his friends. At church on Sunday, after the initial surprised looks, he received a descent number of compliments, he thought.

Knowing that he shared homebase with another teacher, he decided that he would walk in a few minutes after the bell. He wanted to make a grand entrance to the anticipated yelps of delight from his students. Five minutes into the start of homebase, he entered the door. To his shock, embarrassment and hurt, the yelps he heard were of ridicule, put downs, and finger pointing accompanied with laughter.

What shall I do? What shall I say? How should I react? All of these questions went through his mind in rapid fire. Put yourself in the position of this teacher. There are many, many ways that he could react. Stop reading for a moment. Say to yourself softly or out loud what you would do. Of course speculation is easy, but try it anyway. It's a good exercise that might reap benefits later in your professional life.

Okay, back to our young man. He decided to join the revelry. He strutted around the room saying, "Yeah take a look, it's me. I've left the time warp, and I'm all the way live in '95." The students howled with laughter. Soon some of the students became serious and complimented him on his new hair style. The comment that caught his attention and let him know that he had chosen the "correct" action (not the only "correct" action) was when one of the boys gave him a high five and told him that his new haircut stunk, but that he was a great guy.

The second homebase teacher saw the whole episode and was absolutely furious with the teacher and the students. She addressed the teacher later, but she immediately addressed the class. She spoke to them sternly about respecting the feelings of others, about put downs and how they can hurt. She asked them to put themselves in the teacher's place and share what he might have felt. Soon the room became quiet. And almost as if they had all come to the same conclusion, the students began to blurt out apologies. She knew that her reaction was "correct" when a student came up to her and thanked her for helping them realize their error. Other students in the background gave verbal and non-verbal agreement. What would you have done?

"Smile and the whole world smiles with you," is great advice for any teacher (especially teachers who teach in urban schools). Add to that advice that you should learn to "laugh at yourself first and laugh while others are laughing with and at you." Laughing done as a result of humorous situations can be therapeutic as well as curative.

One of the most underrated human qualities that can be essential to successful teaching is the art of humor. Many potentially disastrous situations have been changed positively or at least neutralized by a bit of well-placed humor. It has been my experience that given the opportunity to laugh, students tend to release tension, become more tolerant, re-set their pressure point, and generally become more approachable.

It may come as a surprise to you, but many children in urban areas have never learned to laugh for the sheer joy of laughter. Too often their laughter is humorous ridicule of their peers. Laughter is often associated with pain for many of these children. They laugh when one peer puts down another. They laugh when someone is put down for the clothes they wear. They laugh when they have seen a physical confrontation and the winner (sometimes the loser) laughs and diminishes the severity of it (even if someone was hurt). They laugh when they have seen something that someone else believes they should not have witnessed. There are many occasions when urban children laugh when the more normal reaction may have been to cry, run away and hide, or just scream for the fear and terror of some situations.

Just imagine, you very well may be the one to teach children the art of humor and the joy of laughter. By precept and example, you can "teach" your students that humor can be used to bring fun to a situation, can be constructive, and is a valuable asset that adds to the quality of life and enjoyment.

In reference to the profession of teaching, a good smile and hearty laugh can be a strong tool to have in your school success kit. Humor can be an asset in the classroom with your students and as a part of your basic school demeanor. With all of the pressure and potential for negative possibilities that can surface in an urban school, it is an exercise of wisdom to have a ready smile and a willingness to let a good laugh rip. Don't be so serious-minded that you don't experience the "funner" (term used by urban students to indicate a lot of fun) side of teaching.

RECOMMENDATIONS

- In your quest for "knowing" (Chapter 1), put into your process, questions that will uncover the humor consciousness of your students.

- Provide laughable moments for your class.

- Always be prepared to laugh at yourself.

- Be sure that you are ready to give explanations for when laughter is inappropriate. Have sound, believable reasons for your students.

- Give points when students use laughter correctly with skill. (Develop a reward program). This gives them the freedom to exercise the joy of laughter.

- Make an overt effort to teach students the proper use of humor and laughter. Try to correct in the minds of the students that humor is not a synonym for put-downs. Reward the use of good, wholesome humor.

- Enjoy and exercise your freedom to laugh and use humor as a vital aspect of your teaching.

Chapter V

Those Dog Days

THOSE DOG DAYS

Most of the recent literature published on the subject of education concentrate, and rightly so, on the learner (the child). This chapter, however, will focus on teachers.

Let us briefly explore the need that teachers have for each other. Of course we all know that the best source of information and support comes through teacher to teacher interaction. Unfortunately, teachers don't use their colleagues enough to the benefit of their teaching. Often, teachers use their valuable collegial time registering complaints, sharing frustrations (not to be confused with the one teacher sharing frustrations while the other is giving sound pedagogical advice). In short, a lot of time that is spent among colleagues can only be categorized as B_______________ sessions (rhymes with ditch). In effect, we as professionals sometimes get so involved with the struggle of teaching in urban schools that we fail to get the full value of the knowledge, experience and expertise of our fellow teachers.

Ron Edmonds declared that we (urban educators) have the talent and know-how to educate all of our children. He stated that we will when we get serious enough and decide to do so. A part of that getting serious is mining the precious gold nuggets that are within the minds of teachers (new and seasoned alike).

Most of us become teachers because of some inspirational "teacher" (not necessarily a school teacher) and we usually start our teaching career with a particular teaching style or teacher prototype in mind. Even though we may not have reached this conclusion, to a degree, our success rests on the interface with other teachers. Some teachers serve as classic examples of the type of teacher not to become, but the vast number of teachers have unique methods and techniques as well as outstanding little tricks (FIFTH ACE) that really work. These nuggets lie dormant or go unused. No one asks to know more about them or they simply are not shared.

No one person knows it all. The fact is, the strength and quality of education is literally built on the collective knowing of its practitioners and benefactors. So then each teacher must strive to make sure that he/she becomes a committee of one to promote networking of ideas and practices among teachers. The goal here should be three-fold:

- To open the lines of communication among colleagues;
- To elevate the practice of teaching through the sharing of effective teaching techniques;
- To provide a means of help for teachers in need of professional guidance. That help should be given

in a non-threatening teacher-driven forum within the school.

New teachers, especially, should have not only one, but many teachers in the building as well as within the district (across grade levels) with whom they can share concerns and ask questions. If sharing is a norm in the school, the threat of being thought of as a failure or as incompetent is virtually nonexistent. This kind of academic atmosphere will be wholesome for all teachers and will without question positively affect the students. An atmosphere of open sharing and support among colleagues has the potential to reform the curriculum, develop a problem-solving process, re-think student discipline techniques, and address a host of other issues that normally plague public urban schools. There can be little argument that such a networking process would be invaluable to the school community.

What's wrong with one teacher seeking advice from another? Of course the answer is nothing, nothing at all. The real truth, however, is that there is an unspoken code that says too many questions or asking for help too often probably is an indication that the person is a poor teacher and possibly will not last long. Networking should be, and I hope after reading this chapter you will start to make it, a common and encouraged aspect of teaching. "...Ask and it shall be given unto you." Don't ask and you get nothing. Or as it might be said by urban student language, "Ain't nothing to it, but to do it - ask." There should be no fear or shame associated with trying to gain knowledge. After all, it is a SCHOOL, isn't it? ... A place where ignorance (not knowing) is defeated by knowledge. Ask! Ask! Ask!

One little warning. It is very important who you seek information from that you plan to use in class. Observe your potential advisor when with students in teaching and non-teaching circumstances. Remember, you are not obligated to use the advice at the time it is given (good information will hold). If you cannot see yourself pulling it off, do not try to use the advice until you can see yourself doing it. Look for peers with whom to share, to grow, and to learn as you develop your professionalism. Remember, anybody can groan, place blame, complain, and gossip. BE A PROFESSIONAL!

RECOMMENDATIONS

- Ask! Ask! Ask!

- Share! Share! Share!

- Don't hesitate to ask parents, community people (agencies, institutions, recreation centers, etc.), or any other people who you feel have information that will help educate students.

- Ask the correct person(s) the proper question(s) and/or for advice. For instance, if you have a question about African-American culture, ask a representative of the culture. If you have a question about an Asian student, seek out a representative of the culture to ask your question. That is not to say that others may not be able to answer your question, but it makes more sense to seek a common source first. If you don't get an answer, you will probably at least get the benefit of their insight. This can be a way to start to tear down some of the walls that separate cultures and ethnic groups in urban schools.

Chapter VI

A Final Word

A FINAL WORD

Teaching is a noble and honorable profession. The nobility and honor of teaching are only as stable and true as are those who choose and practice in the profession. If urban teachers are to be looked upon as members of that nobility, it is incumbent upon them to exemplify the highest standards of professionalism and continually seek the best practices and pedagogy in teaching.

It is no secret that teaching in an urban school is challenging to the expertise of teachers as well as to their creative ability. Teachers must not, however, fall victim to the idea that the challenges are insurmountable. Often, urban educators are their own worst enemy and the worst enemy of the reputation of urban education. Teachers who teach in urban schools tend to speak more negatively than positively about the school, their fellow colleagues, the students, the parents, and community. With this constant negative description and negative talk always being the essence of their discussion about their teaching experiences, there is no wonder others feel free to speak in the same negative vein.

In the old community where I grew up, we had kind of an unspoken philosophy. It seemed that everybody knew it and most abided by it. The philosophy was simple and to the point. If you had something or were involved in something that may have been considered by your peers as substandard, or made you the target of ridicule, but it was something that you liked and wanted to remain involved in, or wanted to keep (of course in some cases you didn't have a choice because your parents had already chosen for you), you applied the philosophy. Now the philosophy was to simply find everything good about the thing and then tell those good things to everybody you had occasion to speak to about it. You had to be both bold and brave. At first, everybody would try and sway you from your saying good things position. If you held out and continued to highlight those good things, to your amazement it wouldn't be long before other people would agree with you. In most cases the ones who spoke most negatively at first would even join you in praising whatever the thing was.

One example of having used the philosophy when I was a child stands out in my mind. In my day, everybody hated black and white saddle oxford shoes. If we saw somebody with some oxfords on, we would laugh and make fun of them. It seemed that parents loved those shoes. Even when you didn't want them, they would be the shoes of choice for parents. Of course we knew why...they would never wear out. You either had to throw them out or give them away when they got too small. One pair of saddle oxfords could go through a whole family of children, boys and girls!

One summer my mother decided that because I was so hard on shoes she would buy me some saddle oxfords. She bought them and informed me that they would be my school shoes in September. I was frantic, but I knew the unspoken philosophy. So a few weeks before school started, I invited some of my friends to go window shopping. When we got to the shoe store that had the saddle oxfords in the window, boy did I rave about those shoes! Everybody laughed at first and told me how crazy I was. They were right, I was crazy, but crazy like a fox! Every time one of the girls would point out something wrong or ugly about the shoes I would counter with something good about them. I finally ended the discussion by saying that I was going to ask my mother to buy me some of those shoes as soon as possible. I wanted to be sure to get them before they were all gone. I wanted to wear them to school in September. A few days later, I brought up the conversation again. The girls saw that I was serious and were not as strong in their attack this time. A few weeks later some of the girls confided in me that they thought the shoes weren't so bad and were thinking of asking for some themselves. To make a long story short, by the time school started, most of the girls had the shoes and bragged about them with pride. Needless to say, we set the fashion trend for that school year to the glee of many parents.

As urban educators, we know that the general opinion and view of urban schools by most people is negative at best. I am merely suggesting that teachers do not need to add to that perception. If you have chosen to teach in an urban school, it seems to me that you would be eager to accentuate the positives, if for no other reason but that you are there approximately 180 days out of 365. Sure, everything is not good and perfection in urban schools (in fact, things are not all good and perfect in any school), but there are some good and fantastic things happening in urban schools. Remember that this institution is good enough to afford you an adequately comfortable living, so before you speak ill, remember how you pay the bills!

In a session designed for new teachers, the question was asked if there were things that teachers actually should not say. After much give and take discussion, even debate the answer was 'yes.' Yes, there are things that teachers should not say. Of course, the next obvious question was, "What are some of them?" I would like for you to make your own judgment about them, so I will just include those that were given in that particular teacher training session.

A List of "Never Say" For Teachers

- These kids just don't want to learn.

- I don't know why I'm wasting my time with these kids.

- You know how these people are.

- None of them are any good, they'll probably end up in jail or dead.
- The parents are as bad as the kids.
- None of these teachers care about these kids.
- These students are not worth the effort.
- The parents don't care about their own children.
- These children all come from pitiful homes.
- All these kids know how to do well is curse and fight.
- Most of these kids are on drugs or having sex.
- These children have no morals or values.
- Academic standards have to be lowered so that these kids can pass courses.

There were more, but I think that this is enough to make the point. The low part of this discussion for me was when the question was asked of these new teachers, if they had actually heard these statements made by teachers. The answer was a resounding YES!

One has to ask the question that if teachers feel the way that these comments suggest that they do, how can they effectively work with their students or inspire them in any way?

Just like doctors have a sense of protection for their profession and their fellow doctors, teachers must learn the value and importance of that kind of code. To lose the public trust would be devastating to the medical profession and that is a major factor which motivates doctors. The lack of this same motive has to a large degree been the undoing of teaching, and urban teaching in particular. The public has lost trust in the ability of public schools to educate the young, and they feel that it is true, more especially, about urban schools.

What are we to do? Is all lost? No, teachers must regain the trust of the public. One very small step that teachers could make would be for them to speak with passion and commitment about their craft no matter when they choose to practice it. Urban educators must not be snared by the words of their mouths. If teachers' hearts can believe it and their minds can conceive it, then their mouths should be able to speak it. Out of the abundance of the heart does the mouth speak. It might do the profession of teaching a world of good to have a day where educators across this nation would reaffirm in their own hearts, their personal reasons for teaching.

As you read this book, you may have been moved to think or comment that the examples, discussion and recommendations could be of value in any school. What a welcome revelation. You are perceptive and very correct. I have found that what is good for urban students is actually good for all students. The critical difference is that other students may survive without them. On the other hand, urban students' survival depends on the few recommendations offered here, and the volume of intelligence given by a vast number of authors (refer to the Suggested Readings section).

Your effectiveness as a teacher rests not only on your knowledge of the curriculum, but also on your ability to understand and interpret the words and actions of your students. Learn the culture of the school from the perspective of the adults in the school, the community that includes parents and the students. Take time to observe the students in class, in the halls, at lunch, outside before and after school, and where possible, when they are involved in community activities. Learn to use your imagination and put trust in your intuition. The combination of these experiences will assist you in developing your own unique style for teaching in an urban school. Do not get set in that one style, but continue to explore, observe, and share. The more you know, the more you can grow as an educator. Make it your business to KNOW.

Don't waste you time defining the exorbitant number of conditions and circumstances that urban students face that would cause or justify failure. Yes, it is good to empathize with their plight, but you must not neglect or confuse your role and purpose for being in the school. Spend you time helping them develop excellent competitive academic skills and support them in building a belief system that helps them mentally grasp the possibilities for success in their lives. If you feel it necessary to extend yourself beyond the classroom or seek additional help for your students in order to do that, then do those things. You are sure to make mistakes, but don't be thrown by them. Recognize and acknowledge them, correct them if they are correctable, seek advice if you need it, and continue to teach. Set your face as flint and don't be deterred from your goals. Success is almost a certain guarantee if you will do your best to give your best.

Take this last bit of advice. It is also important that you maintain your mental and physical health. Do not get so involved in what you want to accomplish for students that you forget to include your own health and welfare in the program. Make every effort to keep yourself inspired. Looking into the face of reality day after day can skew your perception and warp your world view which can lead to insensitivity and negative reward. It is of value to have daily reality checks coupled with a dose of "Why am I here?" and "Am I being effective?", conversations with yourself. You need to take a little time every day to pamper and encourage yourself. Think on the success you've had with a particular student, or some great lesson you taught, or the magnificent "Fifth Ace" you played today. Make yourself laugh; don't be afraid to laugh at yourself. Don't let yourself develop or even entertain the victim mentality. If you feel that you have been victimized by the students or victimized because of the school in which you've been placed, remember the philosophy of my childhood and apply it. When life hands you lemons, take out a pitcher, squeeze them, add water and sugar to taste, and make lemonade.

Go in there and teach! Embrace the challenge to be an example of excellence.

Appendix:

Extra Stuff

The kind of "stuff"
succcess in teaching relies on!
Perhaps one day, you might
try one of these as a
"Fifth Ace".

EXTRA STUFF

A Dozen Most Commonly Asked Questions About Urban Schools

Q What assumptions should I make about my students prior to meeting them?

A None. Take the time to read as many books and magazines as you can that will give you cultural knowledge and insights about urban living and the people living in urban areas. This will diminish the possibility for error and misunderstandings. What you learn through your reading will either prove true or false; it may be that you will end up ignoring or rejecting this knowledge due to the experiences you'll have with your students.

Q Why do urban children misbehave so much in school?

A The fact is that urban children don't misbehave any more or less than other children. They simply have different life experiences and sets of expectations. It may be that some children are not aware that they are misbehaving; to them it may be play or the way to protect their space. Under the direction and guidance of a culturally aware teacher, most urban classrooms can be and will be orderly places of learning. Set high goals. Explain and model the desired behavior (it could be that the children have never been expected to behave in the way you are requiring of them. You may be presenting them with a new experience. Don't assume that they know what you want or how to perform it.) If you believe that they can behave properly and that you can teach them, then you will do it.

Q What can I do to make my job easier?

A Anything you can do that helps your students find satisfaction in learning...the more you do for yourself. Student success breeds involvement and peace.

Q Is cooperative learning good for urban children?

A Yes, if done correctly and with total commitment. Urban children are accustomed to doing almost everything with someone and usually in partnership. When they come to school, it is called cheating or misbehaving. Cooperative learning is a sound, cultural modality of learning for urban children.

Q I feel so sorry for these children and really want to help them so badly. Am I wrong to feel this way?

A No, in fact those feelings in proper perspective are excellent motivation for teaching. Part of teaching is a kind of missionary work (no matter where you teach), but only a very tiny part. If you care that much, care enough to do all you can to be an effective teacher.

Q Do most urban black kids feel that white people are bad or racists?

A Some children do feel this way, some don't, and others have not formulated a position. What is significant in reference to race, is that you must not play to the belief that you as a white person (or any other race) are indebted to your students for actual or perceived transgressions. You must be sensitive to their feelings and beliefs. Strive to bring a multicultural perspective to your classroom.

Q What do you do when your colleagues are threatened by your ideas and enthusiasm? Do you just conform to the norm to survive in peace?

A Just remember what is popular is not always right and what is right is not always popular. To thine own self be true!

Q Are white children in urban schools captives to their circumstances in terms of poverty?

A No, not any more than any other urban child. The majority of white children who attend urban schools are residents of the school district just like their counterparts. These children should be respected and treated according to their urban experiences just as other urban children should be.

Q Some black children call each other nigger. Is this an accepted term of endearment?

A In spite of what some young black people may say or think, "nigger" is not an accepted term nor considered proper. As a teacher, you should exercise zero tolerance for this word being used in your presence ever. There is never a proper time or circumstance for the term to be used. If you note your students using this term, this is an indication to you that they need to be taught better (if you feel uncomfortable addressing this topic as a lesson, reach out to others for assistance). It is imperative that the matter be addressed. The answer is no, "nigger" is not a term of endearment nor accepted or acceptable.

Q Why are urban children so brash and rude?

A Think of it this way, not brash and rude, but rather unlearned in the social graces. Don't accept rude and brash behavior as givens. Correct the behavior with what should be the norm. Children are great imitators. What is learned can be unlearned - teach them how.

Q Can I win the respect and affection of urban students?

A Yes, if you earn it. No, if you don't earn it. Set your personal goals and work toward them with your students.

Q I'm a ___________ (subject) teacher. Why must I be concerned with all of these psychological issues and other facets of the lives of urban children? I just want to teach.

A Being in tune with the status of your students will put you in the position to do just that, teach. You must also know your purpose for teaching. You want students to learn. Knowing as much about your students as possible will eventually cause them to embrace the curriculum that you will teach them. You must teach the child, not the curriculum. if you are not effective in causing students to learn, then you are not teaching. You teach people, not concepts.

Q Is teaching in an urban school really different from teaching in a suburban school?

A Yes, it is different to teach in an urban school. Different is not intended to denote any kind of judgement. It is simply a statement of fact. Every school has its own culture. Urban schools have a culture that is developed through the experiences of the school community. Every school has positive and negative features. Unfortunately, urban schools are described more in terms of negative features than other schools. Yes, urban schools are different, but different can be great. It is all in the perspective.

You've Got My Respect

Urban children tend to respect teachers (adults) who exhibit the following:

1) ***Consistency*** - Young people have a need to know the rules and have them acted out consistently by the teacher (adult). Modeling clear standards by teachers (adults) lays a foundation and maps out a path for them to follow. Young people are not totally self-disciplined and rely on the guiding hand of the teacher (adult) to lead the way.

2) ***Equity/Equality*** - Students desire for teachers (adults) to be fair and equal in their treatment of all students. Even the youngest student recognizes and will yield to the teacher (adult) who they see dealing fairly (same way) and equally (to everybody) in all situations. Even if they disagree with the treatment, they will give in to it if they see justice for all.

3) ***Expectations*** - Students may not know how to articulate this desire, but they want teachers (adults) to let them know that they believe in their ambitions, skills and imagination. The theme is YES YOU CAN, I BELIEVE IT FOR YOU. Set

high expectations not just high challenges for your students and yourself.

4) ***Support*** - Students need to know that they will be encouraged to take risks of all kinds. Students need to know that there will always be the teacher to catch them when they fall and rejoice with them in success. Students need a friendly voice, all embodied in a teacher.

5) ***Humor*** - Children of all ages enjoy laughter. They need to have teachers who show them how to laugh and have a sense of humor. Students respect teachers who face challenges with humor and a sense of calm. Smiling is contagious - teachers should be carriers so that they can infect their students.

6) ***Realism*** - Students want to know that their teachers know and are in contact with their reality. They want teachers who make the curriculum relevant and meaningful to their daily lives. They want teachers who are real with them so that they may be free to be real with the teacher.

8 Major Reasons for Misbehavior In School

- Lack of proper rest
- Lack of social skills (no formal way of making friends and/or endearing peers)
- Cover up of the inability to do the assigned class work. When in doubt - act out!
- Driven by the lack of the fulfillment for the need to belong
- The need for attention
- Immaturity
- Short attention span
- Boredom

These are not reasons not to try to teach misbehaving children. With this knowledge, teachers can construct classroom space, develop lessons and be creative in meeting the needs of these students. Every child can learn, you just have to find the proper way to make it happen.

7 Sure Methods To Promote Positive Regard

- ***High Expectations*** (setting reasonable goals and providing the support needed to build confidence in ability).

- ***Structure*** (allow expression of feelings to diminish the feeling of being controlled and permit pent-up emotion to be released therapeutically).

- ***Identity*** (assist them in developing a strong sense of personal identity, "I AM." Acknowledge strengths and support a methodology to cope with weaknesses).

- ***Self-Esteem*** (provide an environment that honors personal worth, value, acceptance, and capabilities).

- ***Sense of Belonging*** (make a conscious attempt to develop an attitude and environment of inclusion, cooperation and non-threatening interaction).

- ***Social Skills*** (develop an atmosphere of mutual respect, consistent rules and boundaries and recognition of small successes).

- ***Tolerance of differences*** (recognizing that all people are unique and of value. Fostering a caring climate that provides positive space for all).

- ***Consistency*** (maintaining a climate that is somewhat routine in schedule, clear expectations for behavior, performance, and recognition of the need to be guided).

Teachers "Shine"

- Strive for Excellence in everything you do. "***SHINE***."
- Hear only those things that are uplifting and encouraging about you and your students. "***SHINE***."
- Involve yourself in the lives of your students as much as you can and in every way you can. "***SHINE***."
- Never give up on your students or yourself. Make your motto - NO LOSSES! "***SHINE***."
- Expel negative myths about teaching in urban schools. Be creative. "***SHINE***."

"SHINE, SHINE, SHINE!!!"

The 10 Biggest Myths

1. Urban children don't value education.

2. Inner-city public schools provide an inferior education.

3. African-American boys need more discipline and corrective action than other students.

4. Home environment hinders a child's ability to be successful in school.

5. Inner-city children tend to respond more positively to firm, inflexible, authoritative treatment by educators.

6. Inner-city children are innately prone to violence.

7. Education is no longer thought of as the key to success.

8. Inner-city teachers are not among the best of the best.

9. Most colleges don't respect diplomas from inner city schools.

10. Parents of inner-city children are not involved in and don't care about their children's education.

JUST A REMINDER

BE SUPPORTIVE

BE RESPECTFUL

BE POSITIVE

BE HONEST

BE TRUTHFUL

BE AN EXAMPLE

BE OPEN-MINDED

COMMON SENSE

HELPFUL HINTS

Common Sense Helpful Hints

Be in charge when you are in charge.

Remember you are an adult; the students are children. Educate, not dominate.

Be creative.

Remember when you were a child? All of those activities and exciting learnings that you enjoyed are equally as valuable today.

Be a cultural name dropper!

No matter what the subject matter, you owe it to students to give it a culturally inclusive foundation.

Be ever alert!

Even when you are not in front of students you are constantly being observed and evaluated by students as long as you are in the building.

Be human and alive.

You are not a buddy, but you should be a friend. Interpersonal relationships can be your most valuable asset.

Be always aware.

Schooling is a continuous process. whatever you bring to the school will become a part of that continuous learning process.

Be yourself, and don't be afraid!

Incorporate the knowledge you gain from the children into a better you.

SUGGESTED READINGS

Akbar, Na'im. The Community of Self (Revised). Florida, 1992.
Angelou, Maya. All God's Children Need Traveling Shoes. New York, 1986.
Angelou, Maya. I Know Why The Caged Bird Sings. New York, 1988.
Asante, Molefi. Malcolm X as Cultural Hero. New Jersey, 1993.
Banks, James. Multiethnic Education: Practices and Promises. Bloomington, 1977.
Brandt, Godfrey. The Realization of Anti-Racist Teaching. Philadelphia, 1986.
Comer, James. Maggie's American Dream. New York, 1988.
Cosby, William (Bill). Fatherhood. New York, 1986.
Fine, Michelle. Framing Dropouts. New York, 1991.
Glasser, William. Control Theory In The Classroom. New York, 1986.
Grant, Carl and Sleeter, Christine. After The School Bell Rings. Philadelphia, 1986.
Hale-Benson, Janice. Black Children: Their Roots and Learning Styles. Baltimore, 1982.
Hare, N., and Hare, J. Bringing the Black Boy To Manhood: The Passage. California, 1985.
Hopson, D., Hopson, D.S. Different and Wonderful. New York, 1990.
Kunjufu, J. Countering The Conspiracy To Destroy Black Boys, Vol. I & II. Illinois, 1986.
Myers, Walter. Brown Angels. New Jersey, 1993.
Nobles, Wade. African-American Families: Issues, Insights and Directions. California, 1979.
Oakes, Jeannie. Keeping Track: How Schools Structure Inequality. Cambridge, 1979.
Rogers, J.A. 100 Amazing Facts About The Negro. Florida (Renewed), 1985.
Sadkor, M. and D. Failing At Fairness. New York, 1994.
Wilson, Amos. Understanding Black Adolescent Male Violence. New York, 1992.

ORDER BLANK

Name____

Address______________________________________

City____________________State______Zip__________

Telephone Number (   ) ________________________

Company or Organization

Name____

Address______________________________________

City____________________State______Zip__________

Telephone Number (   ) ________________________

Add $2.00 per book for postage and handling.

Please send a total of ________ books at the rate of $10.95 per book.

Total # of Books x $10.95 = $________________

Plus $3.00 Postage Per Book ________________

Total Due $________________

Please enclose your check or money order for the total amount due and mail to:

Iris Banister
940 Fernwood Park
Rochester, New York 14609

or call: (716) 224-9945

Thank you for your support.